The DISCIPLES

The lives, stories and careers of
Jesus's most beloved disciples

HOLLY MICHAELS

WESTBOW
PRESS®
A DIVISION OF THOMAS NELSON
& ZONDERVAN

WestBow Press books may be ordered through booksellers or by contacting:

WestBow Press
A Division of Thomas Nelson & Zondervan
1663 Liberty Drive
Bloomington, IN 47403
www.westbowpress.com
844-714-3454

ISBN: 978-1-6642-6573-8 (sc)
ISBN: 978-1-6642-6575-2 (hc)
ISBN: 978-1-6642-6574-5 (e)

Library of Congress Control Number: 2022908280

Print information available on the last page.

WestBow Press rev. date: 9/22/2022

A Note from the Author

Imagine a globe, balancing carefully on the bottom needle and spinning. Now imagine if that globe was made up of billions of little puzzle pieces. Each puzzle piece is a person. And imagine for one moment if one of those puzzle pieces fell out of the globe and disappeared forever. The globe, as God designed, would no longer be complete. It would forever be missing one integral part to finish the whole map.

Humans are unique, bearing the image of God. God carefully designed each of us to be a puzzle piece in His grand design of the world. We are each our own piece, carefully selected, and created to complete a bigger picture. We might only see our piece and wonder where it fits in, but God sees the whole globe and knows when we're missing.

Friends, we are going to dive into a series on the twelve disciples, twelve pieces that fit into a perfect plan for a perfect outcome.

They were a group of misfits, unimportant, unassuming people who Jesus hand-selected to follow Him. He also chose you. We're here to dive into their lives, their path with Christ, and how they changed the world. These twelve people, show how in God's plan Jesus came to save us. Hopefully, these words inspire you that you too can be the Lord's disciple in this broken world.

The goal of this book is to share my years of research, encourage you to look deeper into the pages of the Bible, and find some answers and conclusions for yourself. My Bible references are from the New International Version (NIV), the New Living Translation (NLT), the Christian Standard Bible (CSB), and the CSB She Reads Truth (CSB-SRT) version. My observations and conclusions are not all-inclusive or to be regarded as the truth. The conclusions within are compiled from my research and writings by scholars and theologians alike. The purpose is to drive you deeper into a relationship with Christ by learning about Him in a new way—through his twelve closest friends. It has been said you can learn a lot about a man by those he surrounds himself with. So here we are.

Are you with me? Let's get into it.

Jesus's closest friends. The Twelve Disciples

Simon (called Peter)

Andrew, brother of Peter

James

John, brother of James

Philip

Nathanael (also called Bartholomew)

Matthew

Thomas

James, son of Alphaeus

Simon the Zealot

Thaddaeus (also called Judas, son of James)

Judas Iscariot, the traitor

Contents

Prologue

I want to start this book by saying that as we read about these disciples, we're going to learn a few things. We aren't very different from them. We all have families, stories, and emotions that we live through daily. We're all human. Jesus didn't pick superheroes to be his wingmen. He chose people who were inconspicuous, undesirable, and frankly not great people. He chose them and asked them to come along for the journey. Unlike many of us Christians today, every one of these people knew that following Jesus was something much greater than what they were doing at that time. They dropped what they were doing to follow him.

As we learn more about these disciples, we see who they were and see what they were made of. Their example encourages us that we struggle like they do.

Let's look at an overview of the main gospels we will study.

MATTHEW

The book of Matthew serves as a gateway between the New Testament and the Old Testament. Of the four gospels—Matthew, Mark, Luke, and John—Matthew makes the most connections between the New Testament and the Old Testament. Matthew gives us God's entire plan from Genesis to Revelation and refers to Hebrew prophecies sixty times. It's filled with messianic language referring to Jesus as the Son of David and Old Testament references throughout, including fifty-three direct quotations and seventy-six other references. It discusses Jesus's ministry as well as God's plans for Christians, Christ, and the Kingdom (CSB-SRT, 1635).

Looking at the timeline of Matthew, we see that the Gospel of Matthew was written in the first century around AD 60 before the fall of the temple in Jerusalem in AD 70. The events in Matthew take place between 5 BC and AD 33 which includes the life of Christ. Though Matthew's name is not mentioned in the text, the early church unanimously affirmed that he penned the Gospel of Matthew. Many scholars believe that Matthew used the Gospel of Mark in writing his own. If this is true, then Matthew's gospel was written after Mark's, though the date of Mark's gospel is a little bit of a mystery. Around AD 180, Irenaeus claimed that Mark wrote his gospel after Peter's death in the mid-60s. However, Clement of Alexandria, who wrote only twenty years after Irenaeus, claimed that Mark penned his gospel while Peter was still alive.

The first book of the New Testament begins with "An account of the genealogy of Jesus Christ" (Matthew 1:1). This gospel is written from a strong Jewish perspective to show that Jesus truly is the Messiah who was promised in the Old Testament. The Gospel of Matthew also presents eyewitness testimonies of Jesus's ministry and emphasizes certain theological truths.

1. Jesus is the Messiah, the long-awaited King of God's people (Mark 11:9-10, John 12:13, Isaiah 61:1-2, Luke 4:16-24).
2. Jesus is the new Abraham, the founder of a new spiritual Israel consisting of all people, both Jews and Gentiles, who choose to follow him.
3. Jesus is the new Moses, the deliverer, instructor, and mediator of God's people.
4. Jesus is the Immanuel, the virgin-born Son of God who fulfills the promises of the Old Testament (CSB-SRT, 1636).

MARK

Mark gives us a special look at Jesus. This gospel shows us both the divine and human sides of Christ, giving special attention to Jesus's humanity and emotions. Most biblical scholars believe that Mark's was the first gospel to be written of the four and that it influenced some of the writings in Matthew and Luke. It is believed that the Gospel of Mark was written between AD 64 and 68 and was written about Jesus's ministry from AD 30 to 33.

The author of Mark's gospel is anonymous though the author is believed to be John Mark. John Mark was the son of a widow named Mary, in whose house the church in Jerusalem sometimes gathered (Acts 12:12–17 CSB) and where Jesus possibly ate with his disciples at the Last Supper.

Mark wrote his gospel in Rome either just before or right after Peter's martyrdom. Because Mark generally wrote for Roman Gentiles, he explained Jewish customs in-depth, translated Aramaic phrases and words into Greek, used Latin terms rather than their Greek equivalents, and rarely quoted from the Old Testament.

Mark's narrative identifies the focus in the very first verse: "the gospel of Jesus Christ, the Son of God." Mark's emphasis is that Jesus is the divine Son of God as announced by God at

Jesus's baptism (Mark 1:11). Demons recognized Jesus in Mark 3:11 and 5:7, and God reaffirmed Jesus's identity in Mark 9:7. Jesus spoke of His identity in Mark 12:1–12, hinted at it in 13:32, and confessed it directly in 14:61–62. The Roman centurion even confessed it openly in Mark 15:39. Mark's purpose was to summon people to repent and believe in the good news of Jesus Christ, the Messiah (Mark 1:1, 15).

LUKE

Unlike the gospels of Matthew and Mark, which repeat and reflect each other, thirty-five percent of Luke's gospel is original and unwritten material not seen in the other gospels in the New Testament. Some of the new material includes the stories of the births of both John the Baptist and Jesus (Luke 2–3), the retellings of Jesus's childhood and pre-ministry adult life (Luke 2:40–52), a genealogy that reflects aspects of Jesus's ancestry different from Matthew's (Luke 3:23–38), extra information about Jesus's journey to Jerusalem (Luke 9:51–19:44), and a new take on the destruction of the Temple (Luke 21:5–38). Also specific to Luke is the account of the road to Emmaus and the only description of Jesus's ascension into heaven (Luke 24:13–53).

Luke's gospel is believed to have been written around the same time and by the same person who wrote the book of Acts. Considerable evidence points to Luke as the writer of both books, including Acts 1:1–13 which identifies Acts as a sequel to Luke. The events at the end of Acts happened around AD 62–63, indicating that both Luke and Acts were written in the early- to mid-60s. The events in the Gospel of Luke occur from about 5 BC to AD 33.

Chapter 1

SIMON, WHOM JESUS NAMED PETER

———— ✴ ————

The easiest way to get to know the disciples like a friend is to meet them as such. The disciples were human. They loved like we do, made mistakes as we do, and ultimately died for Christ. The disciples can be broken down into three groups of four. Simon Peter (who we will discuss first), James, John, and Andrew are mentioned the most out of the twelve disciples, forming our first group. The second group is composed of Philip, Bartholomew (also known as Nathanael), Matthew, and Thomas. The third group, the least mentioned in the Bible, is made up of James, the son of Alphaeus, Simon the Zealot, Thaddeus (also called Jude), and Judas Iscariot.

I want us to start with Simon Peter, Jesus's best friend. He was a fisherman, a brother, and a disciple. A man of God whose name was changed by Christ Himself.

We find information about Peter only in the first four gospels, and he only appears in the New Testament. He wrote First Peter and Second Peter himself. However, like many of the disciples, we don't know a lot about him from what the Bible gives us.

In John 1:44, we find that Peter's family was originally from Bethsaida in Galilee, but during Jesus's ministry, Peter lived in Capernaum. He lived at the northwest end of the Sea of Galilee where he and his brother Andrew worked as fishermen. They worked in a partnership there, as told in Luke 5:10, with James and John, the sons of Zebedee[1]. All three of these men soon became Christ's disciples. In Corinthians 9:5 and Matthew 8:14, we find evidence that Peter was the son of Jonah (or John) and Joanna, and he was married (Mark 1:30), unfortunately, we do not know the name of his wife. We know Peter is married because Jesus heals Peter's mother-in-law in chapter eight of Matthew, in Mark chapter one and Luke chapter four.[2] We also find out in Acts 4:13 that although Peter has his own business, he had limited formal education.

From family dynamics to lifestyle, we must realize life was undoubtedly difficult in first-century Galilee. The land was occupied by the Romans, meaning taxes were high and life was hard. Peter owned his own fishing boat that he and his brother used to earn their living. Luke 5:1-11 describes Jesus climbing into the boat that "belonged to Simon Peter". Boat ownership indicated wealth. To have a personal boat was rare at this time. Peter most likely had a successful business, and possibly employees that worked under him.[3]

In John 1:44 we see that their home was in Bethsaida, but in Mark 1:29 we are told they lived in Capernaum, where their families shared a house. Historically, the distance between the two cities was only five miles. However, the taxes were different because they lived in different jurisdictions. Bethsaida was located on the east side of the Jordan River, within the territory of Herod Philip, while Capernaum was on the west side, which belonged to Herod Antipas.

In fact, as fishermen, they had to process their fish by air drying or salting before being able to sell them. The main, and most likely only, fish processing facility on the Sea of Galilee was at Magdala, a town in the same region as Capernaum. Fishermen from Bethsaida would have had to bring their fish across territories to be processed, thus incurring a tax at the border—hence the customs house at Capernaum (Mark 2:14). By already living in Capernaum, Peter and Andrew did not have to pay this tax, saving them money.[4] Their wealth had to have come from the careful stewardship of their money.

Because Galilee was part of the Roman Empire, and Capernaum and the surrounding settlements were places of commerce and trade where multiple languages were spoken, we can assume that Peter knew multiple languages. He would have had to be knowledgeable in languages to trade at the docks.

Peter's story with Christ begins at the docks of the Sea of Galilee, but he doesn't stay there. The best friend of Jesus is one of the most written about disciples in the New Testament. Because his story is spread through multiple books, we are given a good idea of Peter's personality. Imagine the kind of influence that Peter had, to be recorded by so many people.

Peter was an actual person, with values and faults. We meet Peter through multiple encounters, giving us a glimpse of his personality through the writings of the New Testament. The Bible depicts Peter as indecisive and unsure but also determined (Galatians 2:11–14; Acts 4:10 and 5:1–10). We are also given the picture of a hasty man who is rash in his decisions, as in Luke 22:33. In John 18:10, we see him as cranky, irritable, and angry.[5] A shortcoming many of us can relate to. The most important thing for you to remember is that Peter was flesh. He often said the wrong things at the wrong times, earning him the nickname "the disciple with the foot-shaped mouth."[6] Isn't it a testament to who Christ is that He would pick people like you and me? Jesus handpicked people like Peter who made mistakes and messed up.

Imagine Peter in today's world. He declared his loyalty to Christ but denied Him three times merely days later. Peter was Jesus's best friend! But Peter was impetuous and was commonly found arguing with or questioning Jesus, even being foolish with what he said or did. In our walk with Christ, we may stumble like Peter, but we travel along the same path. For all that we promise, we fall short. The same applies to Peter. For all that Peter lacked, his unwavering faithfulness and loyalty to his Lord spoke volumes. He is spoken of as the sweetest friend (John 21:15–17). Jesus treasured Peter; Peter was possibly one of the most devoted disciples of Jesus. Jesus draws us nearer to Him intentionally. Even when we stumble like Peter and deny Christ, His hand is always reaching for us.

Peter's strongest personality trait is perhaps his qualities as a leader. Though we have no definitive age for Peter from the Bible, we can at least assume he was between twenty and thirty. Though he is usually depicted as the leader of the disciples, he was not the oldest. John, brother to James, holds that title (dying in 100 A.D. when Peter died between 64-68 A.D.). In Matthew 15:15 and Luke

8:45, Peter is listed as the head of the disciples who question Jesus about a parable, but in Mark 7:17 the same question is posed from a "group of disciples." When we read about the disciples, Peter is most often mentioned first (Matthew 10:2–4; Mark 3:16–19; Luke 6:14–16; Acts 1:13; compare only Galatians 2:9).

One of my favorite things about Peter is his call into ministry. Though the Bible does not give us clarity into Peter's calling into ministry, as the four gospels all tell it differently, it is powerful. Matthew, Mark, and Luke agree that the calling of Simon Peter took place at the Sea of Galilee. In contrast, the book of John places the call of Simon Peter in Judea (John 1:28). In John 1:35, John the Baptist introduced Peter to the "Messiah". However he was called, Peter dropped everything. Peter walked from his life into a new one full of promise for a man he didn't know. He knew nothing about Jesus, yet everything else became insignificant in comparison to the Son of Man. His instant and steady devotion ultimately lead him to his new name.

The meaning of names in the Bible is important. Often times in the Bible God would change a person's name to signify a distinct change in God's covenant with us. That is the meaning of what we see in Simon's name change to Peter.

Interestingly, the first name change was when God made the

original covenant with Abraham in Genesis 17:5. God changes his name from Abram which meant "high father" to Abraham which meant "father of a multitude". This change came when God created the covenant of circumcision with Abraham. Abraham's wife Sarah also saw a name change when God gifted them with children in Geneses 17:15. God changed Jacob's name in Genesis 32:38 from Jacob to Israel after Jacob had taken Esau's birthright. Jacob's new name meant "having power with God".

When Jesus met Peter his name was Simon. When Peter followed Christ, not only did he receive a new life, but he also received a new identity in the form of a name change from Jesus himself. Simon became Peter. "The Rock" on which Jesus would build His church upon.[7] It gives me goosebumps every time I consider Jesus and Peter at this moment. Imagine the joy Peter felt when his name became changed. He might not have understood exactly what Jesus was doing at that moment, but the significance of his name changing couldn't have been lost on him. Jesus changes people. He changed Peter. He can change you.

Throughout the Bible, the disciples are grouped together at different events. However, Peter is specifically referred to by name while the rest of the disciples are most commonly referred to as disciples or apostles. Jesus calling Peter by his name demonstrates their relationship. Jesus knew him.

In Mark 1:36 and Luke 8:45, Peter is called by name whereas the other disciples are mentioned as merely his companions. In Matthew 17:1 and 26:37, Peter is listed by name before the sons of Zebedee. It is significant that Peter is being called out by name. Less than ten verses earlier, Peter is in refusal that he will deny Christ in the garden. His faith proves to be weak in the absence of the presence of Jesus.

Peter displayed the depth of his love for Jesus in Matthew 16:15–18, Mark 8:29, and Luke 9:20. But as we've seen before, Peter's faith wavered. He stepped out of the boat, and when his eyes landed on the storm, he started to sink. When he lost sight of the Lord, Peter fell. He focused on the storm around him and immediately was stripped of his confidence. Matthew 14:22–33 portrays this incident between Peter and Jesus, showing us, (we are mirror images of Peter)[8]. When we lift our eyes off of the shore, when we lift our eyes off of the Lord, we become unbalanced. We stumble and waver. Ultimately, we sink through the waves like Peter. But we have to remember that God's grace extends to us for the moments like this. Even though Peter sank, remember that out of the disciples, Peter was the only one to try.

> When the disciples saw him walking on the sea they were terrified. "It is a ghost," they said, and they cried out in fear. At once [Jesus] spoke to them, "Take courage, it is I; do not be afraid." Peter said to him in reply, "Lord, if it is you, command me to come to you on the water." He said, "Come." Peter got out of the boat and began to walk on the water toward Jesus. But when he saw how [strong] the wind was he became frightened; and, beginning to sink, he cried out, "Lord, save me!" Immediately Jesus stretched out his hand and caught him, and said to him, "O you of little faith, why did you doubt?" After they got into the boat, the wind died down. Those who were in the boat did him homage, saying, "Truly, you are the Son of God." (Matthew 14:22–33 NIV)

Like Peter, we are of little faith. We stand on the sands right next to Jesus and don't feel him. Peter rides in the boat next to Him and doesn't see him. Jesus had deep love for Peter and was with him even when Peter was weak in faith. We are just like Peter; weak in our ability to comprehend the unfathomable depths of Jesus's love for us.

His faith was unsteady when Jesus rebukes him about His death in Mark 8:32-33. His faith wavers when he staunchly denies Christ in Matthew 26:29-75 (Mark 14:66-72 and Luke 22:54-61 as well) in the Garden of Gethsemane. Like a crack in a window lets the dust filter in, the crack in Peter's faith is His love for Christ. Peter stumbled. But he also knew who his Lord was. Jesus's heart was already known by Peter so intimately that it shouldn't be a surprise that Peter was the first one to identify who Jesus was. When Jesus asks who Peter thinks He is, Peter immediately replied, "The Messiah!"

Right after Peter calls Jesus the Messiah in Matthew 16, he denies Jesus's prophesy. He refuses the truth of what Jesus was speaking to him by saying "Never Lord! This shall never happen to you," but Jesus gently reminds Peter that the purpose of His messiahship is not what Peter thinks it is. The purpose of the cross wasn't for the concerns of man, but the concerns of God.

Isn't that what we do sometimes? We have an agenda that we believe the Lord is doing when really His plan is so different from ours. Our ideas prevent us from realizing the depth of the love we receive from Jesus. Peter doesn't realize Jesus's plan. That requires fellowship with Jesus and sacrificing our old self. Jesus asks this of us further down in this same passage with Peter. His famous words, "Whoever wants to be my disciple must deny themselves and take up their cross and follow me." Throughout the narrative of the gospels, Peter seems so close yet so far from Jesus's message. Peter is seen as Jesus's best friend yet his closeness to Christ might be the blindness that keeps him from seeing His purpose.

One of Peter's most well-intended moments is found in the Garden of Gethsemane. He loves his Lord. Jesus is a close and dear friend to him. Their close friendship is mirrored in the relationship Jesus has with two other disciples; James and John. These three were Jesus's closest friends. Perhaps they were closer than the other disciples because of the way they would eventually go on and be the leaders of the growing Church. Peter was renamed from Simon because of how Jesus used him in ministry. He became a stronghold for Christianity to grow from. But when he was under pressure, Peter cracked. His denial of Christ is not found in only one gospel, but in all four -- Luke 22:54–62; Matthew 26:33–35; Mark 14:29–31; John 13:36–38.

The moments before his denial, we find Peter in the courtyard with the disciples and the Roman soldiers there to arrest Christ. In a surge of protection, Peter cuts off a guard's ear. His devotion to Jesus led him to a decision in an act of protection. But Jesus chastised him. Peter chose anger because he wasn't seeing God's plan. Imagine the moment of correction, and the loneliness Peter must have felt. His best friend just informed him he would deny his involvement with Christ not once but three times before the night was over. He was rebuked for attempting to protect him.

Not only that, his best friend was soon to be crucified in a horrifyingly bloody way. It had to have broken Peter's heart; I know it broke mine. Luke 20:61-62 fills my heart with sorrow for Peter. We read that "The Lord turned and looked straight at Peter...and he went outside and wept bitterly". Just think of the weight that was on Peter's shoulders the moment his eyes met Christ's. It must have felt like the end of the line for him. However that is not the end of Peter's story and life. Jesus wasn't done with him yet.

After Jesus rose from the dead, it is recorded that Peter was the first male and the first disciple to see Him after the Resurrection (Luke 24:34). Peter was transformed from a terrified, dejected failure into the leader that Jesus had prophesied from the beginning. We see him at this moment growing into the identity that Jesus gave him.

The incredible story of Peter continues. Christ again appeared to the disciples after His death and resurrection. Much like the very first time Jesus met the disciples, they were fishing. Jesus entrusted Peter from the very beginning to continue in His wake after He was gone from the earth. Peter was the very foundation that Jesus built his church.

In John 21 we see Jesus asks Peter three times if he loves Him. He then says to Peter "Feed my sheep". At the beginning of Jesus ministry he commissions Peter. At the end after the resurrection He confirms that commission. Jesus never stopped using Peter for His glory.

Peter's later life is not described in the Bible. We have to look to other ancient texts to provide us with information on his life, after Christ's Ascension. Peter's letters in the Bible indicate that he traveled with his wife after Christ's death. This leads us to believe that Peter and his wife served as a team and if they had children, they were already grown.

Peter lived up to Jesus's calling for him and led the twelve apostles in expanding the church (Acts 9:32). In Acts 8:4–17 and Acts 9:32–35, we see that he first went to the Samaritans. He then went to Lydda in the Plain of Sharon and then to the Mediterranean coastal town of Joppa (Acts. 9:36–43).[9]

In Acts 10–11:18, Peter traveled north to the Mediterranean coast to Caesarea. There he introduced Gentiles to the church. His work there and the baptism of a large number of people are factors that led to Peter's arrest (Acts 12:2, 3). In prison, an angel of the Lord visited Peter and he escaped (Acts 12:1-8). This is where we find ourselves looking outside of the Bible to other ancient texts, to sum up the rest of Peter's life.

We know that in his final years he traveled to Rome and it was there that he died.[10] Peter was hanged upside down and beheaded in AD 67 at the Circus Maximus during a brutal anti-Christian period under Emperor Nero, which followed the burning of Rome. It is believed that Peter's cruel treatment in his final days was partly the result of his request not to be crucified.[11] Even facing death, his loyalty to his Lord never wavered. He didn't consider himself worthy of the same treatment as Christ. After he died, it is said that his body was laid to rest in a burial ground that is now the site of St. Peter's Basilica. He was the first Pope of the Catholic Church and is known today by Catholics as St. Peter.

Peter's story gives us hope. He believed in the Lord but still faced many trials. He may have denied his faith and failed the Lord.

But Jesus still had plans for him. He could not escape the purpose that Christ had laid out for his life. Through his weaknesses, Jesus turned him into a great person. Take heart, that even if your faith fails you, even if you're sinking in the water, Jesus is walking right alongside you. Be like Peter and fight for the Lord. Keep your faith close to your heart and talk to Jesus like a friend.

REFLECTION QUESTIONS

Peter denied Christ three times even when he claimed to love Him. Have you ever found yourself in a similar position in your relationship with Christ? Do you find yourself denying Christ when He is right in front of you?

Do you see yourself in Peter and his actions? Why or why not?

Life is unpredictable. There are storms and waves that throw us off balance. If you had the courage of Peter, would you step out of the boat in the middle of the storm? What storm can you face right now that you're putting off?

Reflect on Jesus's kindness to Peter. Jesus changed his name from Simon to Peter and named him "the rock" of the disciples. He had great plans for Peter. What does that look like in your own life?

Chapter 2
ANDREW THE PROTOCLETUS, BROTHER TO SIMON PETER

The second disciple in our first group is Andrew, younger brother to Simon Peter. Of the twelve disciples, Andrew is recognized as the first one to become a disciple. He is the biggest evangelist of the twelve disciples, and continually brings people to Jesus time and time again.

There are several different accounts of how Andrew became the first. The Gospel of Matthew claims that Jesus was walking along the shore and saw Peter and Andrew fishing. Jesus called to them and promised to make them fishers of men if they came with Him. The Gospel of Mark tells it similarly, while the Gospel of Luke only mentions Peter directly and Andrew is not mentioned. The Gospel of John includes yet another version. John, Andrew and

Peter are already followers of John the Baptist, Jesus's cousin. John

the Baptist recognizes Jesus as the Messiah and tells his followers

they need to follow Jesus instead of him. Andrew follows Jesus

and drags his younger brother to Christ as well. This is our first

introduction of Andrew's evangelism (John 1:41).[12]

As for Andrew being the first disciple of Christ, some

theologians say it's simply a matter of chronology.[13] But what

matters is that Andrew and Peter became the first disciples. Even

though Andrew isn't one of the main pillars of the church, his

evangelism of the gospel is one of the defining characteristics

of his discipleship. He is only mentioned 12 times in the New

Testament, and four of those times he is listed in the group of

disciples. However the few glimpses we get of him are prominent

examples suggesting he was one of the main apostles.[14]

Andrew's early life details are simple. Andrew in Greek

translates to "manly" or "valor."[15] The significance of Andrew's

name reflected the stature of his nature that God wanted to use.

He was a fisherman, which meant he had to be physically strong

to work outside in demanding conditions.[16] His brother Peter and

his father Jonah (or John) were also fishermen. Andrew was born

between AD 5 and AD 10 in Bethsaida, the principal fishing port of Palestine.[17] His business partner and friend Zebedee, the father of James and John, was also a fisherman.[18]

Andrew was an inquisitive man. Growing up, he would have attended school at the synagogue from the age of five to study scriptures, astronomy, and arithmetic.[19] When he was older, he met John the Baptist on the banks of the Jordan River.[20] In Mark 13, Andrew joins Jesus and his close circle of friends, Peter, James and John, to ask questions about the end times. He was interested in being taught by Jesus, and having deeper knowledge from Christ. His thirst for knowledge drove Andrew to share what he was learning. Later, In John's account of the feeding of the five thousand (6:8-9), we see Andrew bringing people to Jesus. It started with the boy who fed the five thousand with his baskets of bread and fish.

The Gospel of John includes an exciting story that sheds light on Andrew's character and treatment in the Bible. In all four of the gospels, Andrew is barely mentioned by name. He's simply one of the twelve, although some evidence points to the fact that Andrew was one of Jesus's closest disciples. Whenever Andrew is named, it is nearly always in a story about someone coming into a relationship with Christ, just as Andrew did with his brother Peter.

This places Andrew at an essential place, in the seat of evangelism in the Bible.[21]

Let's take a closer look at the relationship between Andrew and his brother Peter. Like any siblings, they probably had arguments and problems with each other. However they had a deep bond, as each of the gospels refers to Andrew as Peter's brother. Let's note that throughout the Bible, Peter is never referred to as Andrew's brother. Historically, the older sibling is always referred to first and the younger brother (Andrew, in this case) is named last.[22]

However, this distinction doesn't mean Andrew was less important. Andrew is only mentioned specifically three times in the Bible. The first is the feeding of the five thousand in John 6, the second is during the destruction of the Temple in Mark 13, and the third is when Jesus predicts His death in John 12:20–36. Andrew didn't have to show up multiple times to teach us something.

In John 12:20–36, Jesus enters Jerusalem before Passover. Some Greeks who believe in God seek out Philip and the other disciples, asking to see Jesus. Philip brings them to Andrew to let him decide how to proceed. Perhaps Philip brought the Greeks to Andrew because Andrew had more authority than the other apostles, because he was closer to Jesus, or because he was trusted to make the best decision. Whatever the reason, this gives us another glimpse of Andrew's person that doesn't appear in the other gospels.

> Now there were some Greeks among those who went up to worship at the festival. They came to Philip, who was from Bethsaida in Galilee, with a request. "Sir," they said, "we would like to see Jesus." Philip went to tell Andrew; Andrew and Philip, in turn, told Jesus. (John 12:20–22)

Foretelling the destruction of the Temple, Jesus tells his disciples, "Not one stone here will be left on another; everyone will be thrown down" (Mark 13:2). Later on the Mount of Olives, Andrew, James, John, and Peter privately ask Jesus when this will happen. Jesus tells them about the end times. All three gospels record this narrative, but only Mark calls the disciples by name. This is one of the strongest arguments for Andrew being in the inner circle of disciples because he is named explicitly with other disciples in that inner circle.[23]

In apocryphal texts outside of the Bible, it is believed that Andrew traveled to the Black Sea after the Crucifixion and Resurrection of Christ.[24] In the city of Synope, it is thought he suffered many hardships, and the house he lived in was nearly burnt to the ground.[25] He returned twice more to Asia Minor and Greece and even traveled as far as Hungary, Russia, and the banks of the Oder in Poland in an attempt to spread the gospel.[26]

In Greece, Andrew forged his way through a forest riddled with wolves, bears, and tigers.[27] In Patras, he was captured and given a choice to sacrifice to the gods or be scourged and crucified.[28] By his request, he was crucified on a diagonal cross.[29] Like his brother Peter, he did not believe himself worthy of an upright crucifixion like Christ's. He hung there for three days, fixed not by nails but by ropes, and preached until he died.[30]

Centuries later, we still remember Andrew by his relationship with his brother Peter and his desire to see others brought to Christ. His passion for truth remains. Other details of his life may be vague and are mostly guesswork, but one thing can be certain: long before Peter claimed that Jesus was the Messiah (Matthew 16:16–20), Andrew announced it first (John 1:41).

> He first found his own brother Simon and said to him, "We have found the Messiah." (John 1:41)

REFLECTION QUESTIONS

Andrew was the first disciple. What do you think it meant to him to be asked to follow Jesus first?

Andrew is written about in the Bible as second to his brother Peter. Where do you find yourself falling second to people or things in your life? How does that affect how you view God?

When was the moment in your life when you found the Messiah? It doesn't have to be a huge moment. Take a moment to write it down, reflect upon it, and jot down a verse or two that takes you back to that moment and feeling in time.

Andrew was the second sibling. Look closely at his relationship with his brother. How does that reflect on his character? What does your relationship look like to your brothers and sisters in Christ?

Chapter 3
JAMES, BROTHER OF JOHN AND SON OF ZEBEDEE

James is the third disciple we will study. One of Jesus's three closest friends, and the first disciple to be martyred for Him.

James was the son of Zebedee and Salome, brother to John, and business partner to Peter. He was born in Capernaum and worked there as a fisherman with his brother for their father on the Sea of Galilee. When Jesus called him to follow Him, James was working with John and Peter simultaneously. The way the Bible approaches James and John's relationship, we can assume that James was the older of the two brothers as he was always mentioned first.[31]

James sees Jesus preaching and becomes a witness to Jesus's teaching and miracles. He is present when Christ appears to the crowds and when Jesus reappears to His disciples after His

Resurrection. James appears twice in the gospels: once to ask Jesus to let them (James and John) sit on either side of him in Heaven, one on the right and one on the left (Mark 10:35–40)—however, Jesus tells them it is not his right to grant and the second to witness Christ's third appearance after His Resurrection.[32] He is also present when the disciples replace Judas Iscariot following his treason and suicide.

James, John, and Peter were considered Jesus's three closest disciples, and they were often found with Jesus doing things or witnessing miracles the other disciples never did. Together they saw Jairus's daughter raised from the dead in Mark 5:37–43. They viewed the Transfiguration in Matthew 17:1–3 and Jesus's agony in the Garden of Gethsemane in Matthew 26:36–37.

> He did not allow anyone to accompany him inside except Peter, James, and John, the brother of James. When they arrived at the synagogue official's house, he caught sight of a commotion, people weeping and wailing loudly. So he went in and said to them, "Why this commotion and weeping? The child is not dead but asleep." And they ridiculed him. Then he put them all out. He took along the child's father and

mother and those with him and entered the room where the child was. He took the child by the hand and said to her, "Talitha koum," which means, "Little girl, I say to you, arise!" The girl, a child of twelve, arose immediately and walked around. [At that] they were utterly astounded. He gave strict orders that no one should know this and said she should be given something to eat. (Mark 5:37–43 NIV)

Much like Peter, James's attitude was not always the best. He was human, after all. He could often be rash and unthinking and did not always apply the gospel teachings to earthly matters. We see this in Luke 9:56 when both James and John get angry at an innkeeper in a Samaritan village and ask Jesus to call fire down from the heavens for revenge. Jesus stops them and says, "the Son of man did not come to destroy men's lives, but to save them." Even as a rebuke, I get chills from this. Jesus was God's Son. He was perfect in every way, and yet he assumed the body and flesh of man. He became human to save all of us. Jesus came to save my life the same way He came to save yours. In the same way that we have to take a moment to absorb this message, so did James and John. They had to learn the purpose of Christ.

James and John often had an enthusiastic zeal for the Lord which earned them the nickname of *Boanerges,* meaning "sons of thunder" in Greek.[33] This zeal for the gospel followed James all through his life, and we find in around AD 44 King Herod Agrippa I of Judea killed him with a sword. He was the first of the twelve disciples to be martyred in the early persecution of the church (Acts 12:2). [34]

> James, son of Zebedee and his brother John (to them, he gave the name Boanerges, which means "sons of thunder"). (Mark 3:17 NIV)

After Pentecost, however, James's name disappears from the gospels. In the years following Jesus's Resurrection, James traveled to Spain and Sardinia to preach before returning home to Jerusalem, though this is not entirely conclusive.[35] We do know that James is the only disciple whose death is recorded in the bible. Herod had him killed in Acts 12:2, and scholars believe his death happened in Jerusalem around 44 AD.[36]

Though we know less about James's life than some of the other disciples, we can still learn a lot from his character. Like James, we can be zealous with love for our Lord no matter our circumstances.

REFLECTION QUESTIONS

James is described as being zealous after God's own heart. In your own relationship with Christ, how would you describe the state of your heart?

Many of the disciples are grouped in with their brothers. What are some ways you can strengthen your relationships with your brothers and sisters in Christ today?

What is your attitude towards Christ? How would you define your process of spreading the gospel? How would you talk to another person about your faith?

Chapter 4
JOHN, BROTHER TO JAMES AND SON OF ZEBEDEE

———— ✺ ————

*J*ohn our fourth disciple is most commonly known as "the disciple whom Jesus loved" (John 13:23). Writings about John can be found in the New Testament of the Bible in five of the twenty-seven books: the four gospels and Acts. Most mentions of him are in the Gospel of Mark, followed by Matthew, and then Luke. He only appears once in the Gospel of John and Acts.

John is the younger brother of James, son of Zebedee and Salome. He was born in modern-day Palestine around the same time as Christ -- around 6 AD.[37] Christian tradition situates John's family in Bethsaida on the shores of the Sea of Galilee.[38] His father Zebedee was a fisherman and his mother Mary (or Salome) is considered the stepsister to Mary, the mother of Jesus.[39]

John was an apostle of Jesus and the author of three letters in the Bible, the fourth gospel, and possibly the book of Revelation. He also played a leading role in the early church in Jerusalem.[40] He was an important person in recorded history.

The life of John closely follows that of James, after Jesus called them into ministry. He is a zealous man, passionate about the Lord and His teachings. In the book of Acts he is portrayed with Peter as a strong and steady companion. John was one of those people that were so passionate about following Christ that he sometimes reverted to violence. We see his violence come out when he is angered by a Samaritan innkeeper who would not accept Jesus in Luke 9:51-18:14. He and his brother demand that Jesus call down fire from heaven onto the city. Jesus, however, proclaims against it. In the Gospel of John, the sons of Zebedee are mentioned only once. They are mentioned at the shores of the Sea of Tiberias, where Christ appeared after He rose.

Peter and John are paired together, sharing several unique experiences before Jesus's death in Luke 22:8. They are described as leaders who perform miracles in Acts 3:1–4 and Acts 3:11. They both go to jail in Acts 4:1–3. They serve as emissaries to the Samaritans in Acts 8:14.

During the second century, many writings regarding John

appeared. Many of these writings associate John with the "beloved disciple" (John 13:23, 19:26, 20:2, 21:7, and 21:20–23). It might seem presemputious of John to be nicknamed the "beloved disciple" or the "disciple whom Jesus loved" but Jesus's love is perfect even with his inner circle of close friends. Charles Spurgen explained this through the washing of feet. Jesus washed all of their feet - including Judas's.[41] There is no limit to Jesus's love. It isn't a well that will eventually dry up. His love is everlasting.

As to why John was referred to as the "beloved disciple", William Barclay wrote that John wouldn't have chosen the name for himself, rather it would have been given to him. The meaning does not cross over into our own culture with what we think about love is. The phrase is perhaps considered to highlight God's love and how it transformed his life, rather than being used as a description of his personality or abilities.[42]

However, the "disciple whom Jesus loved" is never actually named in the Bible.[43] The anonymous "beloved disciple" is based on an eyewitness of Jesus's death (John 19:25) whose testimony supported the gospel in John 21:25. He was an ideal disciple, present with Jesus in His last hours and adopted as His brother at the foot of the cross. He was also a witness to Christ's Resurrection.[44]

John's history is obscure as are some of the other disciples' lives following the Resurrection of Christ. Aside from being present at Jesus's third appearance to His disciples and at the decision to replace Judas Iscariot, John is never mentioned in the Bible again except for the depiction of his death. We can only look to older texts outside of the Bible to piece together his life. But these didn't appear until much later, in the third and fourth centuries following John's death.

Legends circulated after John's death, inspired by the passage in Mark 10:39 with its hints at martyrdom. Tradition says that John spent his last days in Ephesus, banished to the island of Patmos for preaching the gospel (Revelation 1:9).[45] In *Foxe's Book of Martyrs* John Foxe writes that John was sent from Ephesus to Rome where he was cast into a cauldron of boiling oil, but escaped unscathed. The second-century North African theologian Tertullian supported this claim.[46] It was from there that he was then cast onto the island of Patmos to die. His death is recorded around 100 AD, making him the longest living disciple and the only one to die of old age.

Polycrates, bishop of Ephesus at the end of the second century, claims that John's tomb is at Ephesus. He also identifies John as the beloved disciple and adds that he "was a priest, wearing the sacerdotal plate, both martyr and teacher."[47]

Because of the inspired visions of the book of Revelation, the Byzantine church depicts John as "the Theologian."[48] Though this title appears in Byzantine manuscripts, it does not appear anywhere in the gospels.[49]

John was an important disciple. Jesus hand-picked him and chose him as a follower. He served alongside Jesus, witnessed miracles, and most likely performed some himself after Christ's Ascension. Even though his life drifts away from public view and we are left piecing his life together to know more about him, we know that God knew his every step, just like God knows ours.

REFLECTION QUESTIONS

How do you think John's personality affected his ability to effectively spread the gospel?

What do you look like when you are talking to others about God? Do you get defensive? Or do you allow them to speak without interruption and offer love?

How can we love someone even when his or her view is different from our own? Christians are supposedly known by their love, but that's not always true. How can you make that true when you talk to someone about Christ?

Chapter 5

PHILIP

———— ❊ ————

$\mathcal{W}$e find mentions of Philip in Matthew, Mark, Luke, John 1:43, 45–46, 48, 6:5, 7, 12:21–22, and 14:8–9, and Acts 1:13. Philip was born in Bethsaida in Galilee around the time of Jesus's birth and he died in the first century. Like Peter and Andrew, Philip was Galilean from the village of Bethsaida. Peter, Andrew, and Philip were probably all friends with one another.

At the time of his call, Philip was involved with a group of people following John the Baptist, who was teaching that Jesus was the "Lamb of God." Some have speculated that Philip was the first of John the Baptist's followers because they lived in the same area.[50] Jesus was not who Philip, being a Jew, would have expected to be the Messiah. It was John's influence on Philip that led Philip to recognize Jesus for who He was: the fulfillment of the Jewish prophecies, even though Christ was a pacifist instead of a warrior.[51]

Perhaps John's influence led Philip to drop what he was doing and follow Jesus when Jesus called to him and said, "Follow me" (John 1:43). Philip was likely one of the disciples at the wedding in Cana where Jesus performed his first miracle: turning water into wine, though he is not directly mentioned.

Philip was also instrumental in the call of skeptical Nathanael, also known as Bartholomew, whom he brought to Jesus. Philip teaches Nathanael what John taught him about Jesus being the fulfillment of the Jewish prophecies. He sought the path to salvation which led him to Jesus Christ.

Jesus even revealed to the disciples later that He supernaturally saw Nathanael sitting under a fig tree before Philip even called him to follow Jesus (John 1:46–50).[52] Nathanael is amazed and instantly believes that Jesus is the Messiah, showing his all-or-nothing attitude.[53]

Philip also participated in the miracle of the loaves and fishes in John 6:5–9. Jesus tested him here and asked him where they could get enough loaves of bread and fish to feed the five thousand men. Historically, the Bible only counts the men who were there, not the women or children. There could have been close to ten thousand or more people.[54] Imagine Philip's surprise at the question. Jesus was asking him a question we all know had more importance than the answer. Philip responds to Jesus with his limited earthly knowledge by saying that eight months of wages would not feed all the people there. He was right. But that's not how Jesus works.

Philip is only mentioned a few more times in the New Testament. We see him in John 12:21–22, where he, along with the Apostle Andrew, brings word to Christ that Greeks are asking to see him.

The last time Philip is mentioned is the most memorable for me. We see him again in the Gospel of John when Philip struggles to know the significance of Jesus. In fact, on one occasion Philip asks Jesus to reveal who the Father is but receives this answer instead:

> "Have I been with you so long, and yet you do not know me, Philip? He who has seen me has seen the Father." (John 14:8–9 NIV)[28]

Philip's struggle with recognizing Jesus as the Messiah is one we all identify with. Don't we also struggle to see Jesus even when he is right in front of us? Philip's struggle is close to our hearts.

We don't know much more about him in the New Testament as

he is not mentioned again. There is a brief reference to Philip the Evangelist, who is presumed to be the disciple Philip, in Acts 6:5. Tradition tells us that Philip preached in Phrygia in Asia Minor and then was martyred by hanging in Hierapolis.[55]

Philip fervently sought after the Messiah, a lifelong journey. He recognized that Jesus was the promised Savior but didn't fully realize it until after the Resurrection. Starting with John the Baptist, Philip sought the path to salvation, which led him to Jesus Christ and the way of everlasting life that came with Him.

REFLECTION QUESTIONS

Philip believes in Christ when he sees Him, even though that belief goes against the teachings of his childhood. The Christ he meets is not the Christ he was taught about. Where have you faced a similar situation in your life? Have you met a different version of God than the one preached about in the world?

Philip helped bring Nathanael to Christ by teaching Nathanael what he learned from John. How is the repetition of teachings instrumental in spreading the Christian faith? Do you teach others what you learn?

Jesus asks Philip if he recognizes him in John 14:8–9. How many times a day do we fail to recognize what Christ is doing? Make a list of a few times you've seen, felt or heard Christ in your life today.

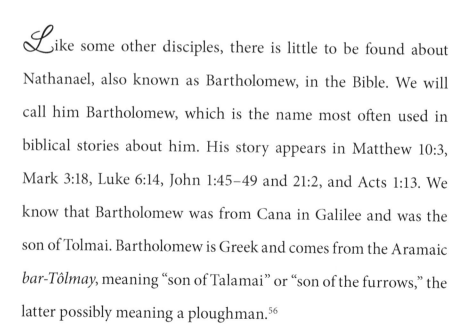

Chapter 6

NATHANAEL, ALSO KNOWN AS BARTHOLOMEW

———— ❉ ————

*L*ike some other disciples, there is little to be found about Nathanael, also known as Bartholomew, in the Bible. We will call him Bartholomew, which is the name most often used in biblical stories about him. His story appears in Matthew 10:3, Mark 3:18, Luke 6:14, John 1:45–49 and 21:2, and Acts 1:13. We know that Bartholomew was from Cana in Galilee and was the son of Tolmai. Bartholomew is Greek and comes from the Aramaic *bar-Tôlmay*, meaning "son of Talamai" or "son of the furrows," the latter possibly meaning a ploughman.[56]

In the New Testament, we find out how Bartholomew came to meet Christ. One of my favorite things about Bartholomew's coming to Christ is how it happens. A friend helping a friend.

Philip, Bartholomew's friend, is the one to tell him about Christ. Bartholomew is skeptical at first, as are several of the other disciples (John 1:43–46). But when Bartholomew first meets Christ, we find that Christ already knows who Bartholomew is. Imagine meeting a person for the first time and they can tell you everything about yourself. Including things, you didn't even know yourself. This is Bartholomew's meeting with Jesus. Jesus knows him and sees him sitting beneath a fig tree (John 1:48). In Judaism, the fig tree is a symbol of the law (the Torah) and in the literature of the Torah, the correct place to study is under a fig tree.

If we look carefully at the moment Bartholomew met Jesus, we see that Jesus called him a man of integrity and admired his openness to the work of God. Jesus isn't referring to his physical nature here, he's referring to what he saw in his heart (Hebrews 4:12-13). Jesus called him a "true Israelite," identifying Bartholomew with Jacob, the father of the Israelite nation (John 1:47) Imagine if Jesus identified your heart with the father of the Israelite nation. Can you imagine the power Jesus's words had over Bartholomew's heart? Just picture the life that was breathed into his heart at this moment. The King of Kings is blessing Bartholomew with his words!

Bartholomew's shining moment in the Bible is that he is the first recorded person in the Bible to profess his faith in Jesus as his savior. When Philip brings him to Jesus, Bartholomew is skeptical (John 1:43–51).

> "How do you know me?" Nathanael asked. Jesus answered, "I saw you while you were still under the fig tree before Philip called you." Then Nathanael declared, "Rabbi, you are the Son of God; you are the king of Israel." Jesus said, "You believe because I told you I saw you under the fig tree. You will see greater things than that." He then added, "Very truly I tell you, you will see 'heaven open, and the angels of God ascending and descending on the Son of Man." (John 1:46-50 NIV)

Jesus tells Bartholomew here that despite his skepticism, Bartholomew would be privy to some of the most incredible miracles, including the resurrection and ascension of Christ. In Acts 1:4, 12, and 13 we see this played out, as Jesus described. On each of these occasions, Bartholomew is mentioned in the company of Philip, and in the gospel of John he is called Nathanael instead.[57] He is also mentioned by the name Nathanael in John 21:2 at the

Sea of Galilee with the other disciples after Jesus's Resurrection, this suggests he is one of the original twelve.[58]

Following the Resurrection of Christ, Bartholomew became a missionary, traveling to spread the gospel. We are not completely sure how he died, but legend has it that he was flayed alive and crucified upside down like Peter.[59] It is said he converted Polymius, the king of Armenia, to Christianity, and because of that, Polymius's brother Astyages ordered Bartholomew's execution.[60] Other sources suggest Bartholomew was beheaded instead.[61]

However he died, Bartholomew shows us that our prejudices can easily skew our judgment. By allowing ourselves to be open to God's word, we welcome in and recognize the truth. By looking at Bartholomew's response to Jesus, we can see how a true believer should respond to Christ every single time.

REFLECTION QUESTIONS

Philip led Bartholomew to Christ and introduced them. There are times in our lives when something seems like happenstance but it is ultimately part of the greater plan. Describe a time something similar to this happened to you and changed your life.

Jesus knew Bartholomew before he knew Christ. How intimate of a relationship Christ seeks with us! He knows you now, every piece of you. How can you know Christ intimately? What can you change in your daily walk to draw you closer to Him?

Identify three truths the world tells us about Jesus and three truths the Bible tells us about Jesus. Write down the Bible verses and compare. What does the world tell us? And what does the Bible tell us? How likely are you to believe one truth over the other if you encounter it in your everyday life?

Chapter 7
MATTHEW THE TAX COLLECTOR, ALSO CALLED LEVI

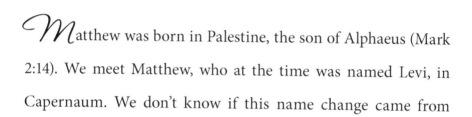

$\mathcal{M}$atthew was born in Palestine, the son of Alphaeus (Mark 2:14). We meet Matthew, who at the time was named Levi, in Capernaum. We don't know if this name change came from Jesus or if Matthew changed his name, but the shortened form of Mattathias, which means "gift of Yahweh" or "the gift of God," became Matthew.[62]

Our first meeting with Matthew in the Bible is when he is in Capernaum, sitting in his tax booth on the main highway, collecting duties on imported goods brought by farmers, caravans, and merchants. He was employed by Herod Antipas, the tetrarch of Galilee at the time.

As a tax collector, Matthew would have been fluent in Aramaic and Greek because of his need to converse with all people.[63] The way the tax system was laid out during this time meant that many tax collectors were corrupt.[64] Under the issue of the Roman Empire, Matthew would have paid all the taxes before he collected them from citizens to reimburse himself.[65] A lot of tax collectors extorted people for more than they owed, all for personal profit.[66] Because Roman soldiers were supporting tax collectors, no citizen dared object.[67]

On the same day Jesus invited Matthew into ministry with Him, Matthew threw a large banquet for Him in Capernaum so his friends could meet Jesus too (Luke 5:29–32). We aren't sure of the reasons why Matthew threw the banquet, to begin with, however, we know that after the banquet, Matthew was a changed man. Instead of collecting taxes, Matthew collected souls for the kingdom of God. Matthew was uniquely qualified to become a disciple despite his sinful past. He was attentive to detail and a keen observer. These attributes served him well when he wrote the Gospel of Matthew some twenty years later.

Matthew also knew the longing of the Jewish people's hearts. He paid attention to people. Of the four gospel writers, Matthew presented Jesus to the Jews as their long-awaited Messiah. His account and writings in the book of Matthew are tailored to answer all of their aching questions.

We cannot know for sure what the rest of Matthew's life entailed. Tradition says he preached for fifteen years following Christ's Resurrection in Jerusalem and then, like the others, served in other countries as a missionary.[68] We do not know precisely how he died; some theologians say he died of old age. Others believe he was martyred with a halberd (a combination of a spear and battle-ax) in the city of Nabadar.[69]

However he died, he displayed one of the most radically-changed hearts in the Bible. Matthew accepted Jesus's invitation to follow Him unwaveringly. He did not hesitate or look back. His life of wealth and security was abandoned for the promise of holy eternity with Christ. He abandoned his wealth and pleasures for the promise of eternity.[70] He was an eyewitness to the Savior, a detailed recorder of Jesus's life and the story of His birth, and a missionary who continued to travel and preach about the good news of salvation.

If you need any evidence that God can use anyone to do His work, Matthew is it. If He can use someone as lowly as a tax collector, then surely He can use us. We should not feel unqualified because of our appearance, lack of education, or what we've done in the past. Jesus searches for heartfelt commitment. Our highest calling in life is to serve God, no matter what the world tells us. Money, wealth, fame, power, and influence are all temporary and cannot compare to the rich glory awaiting us in following Jesus Christ.

REFLECTION QUESTIONS

Why do you think Jesus chose Matthew, a known sinner, thief, and conniver?

One of my favorite people in the Bible is Matthew. He went from being a tax collector to being a servant of Christ. We are witness to his heart change as he goes from sinful to saved. If we wrote ourselves in as Matthew, what would our journey look like?

Matthew dropped everything to follow Christ, without considering the consequences. Do you find yourself dropping everything to follow Christ's calling on your life? Where are you hesitating?

Chapter 8
THOMAS ("DOUBTING THOMAS")

———— ✳ ————

*T*homas was born in Galilee and died around AD 53 in Madras, India. His name is both Aramaic and Greek and means "twin." John 11:16 identifies Thomas as "Thomas, called the twin." He is also called Judas Thomas, or twin Thomas, by the Syrians.[71] It is unclear why he was named that or even who his twin was (John 11:16, 20:24, and 21:2) as the Bible never tells us.

Thomas's character and story are written in the gospel of John. He is a minor character, but don't let that fool you. The verses we find him in are of utmost importance. The phrase "doubting Thomas" comes from this man because of his questions to Christ. His story begins in John 11:5–16. Jesus is planning to return to Judaea when His disciples warn him of the people's desire to have

Jesus stoned. Thomas tells Christ, "Let us also go, that we may die with him." At the Last Supper, Thomas cannot understand what Jesus means when He says,

> "I will come again and will take you to myself, that where I am you may be also. And you know the way where I am going." (John 14:1-7 NIV)

Thomas's question "How can we know the way?" spurs Jesus's response: "I am the way, the truth, and the life." Thomas asks the most important question any of us can think of. Jesus answers it with patience and love. He is the only way. Thomas is a witness to this when in John 11:16 he sees Jesus raise Lazarus from the dead. Only Christ could do the inconceivable.

Perhaps his most famous interaction in the Bible is where we get his name "doubting Thomas". We see this story in John 20:19–29. Thomas is not one of the disciples to see Jesus the first time He appears to his disciples after the Resurrection. When the disciples tell Thomas that Jesus has risen from the dead, he doesn't believe them. I mean, who would? He watched Jesus die. He was there. His disbelief at Christ being alive again would be a hard pill to swallow for anyone.

Thomas wanted physical proof that Christ was alive. When Christ appears and tells Thomas to touch his physical wounds, Thomas realizes the truth, saying, "My Lord and my God!" in John 20:28. How overpowering and awestruck this moment must have been for Thomas. He sees his Lord, alive and well. He bears the marks of sin paid for on His hands. And Thomas gets to touch the very hands that hold everything in them. This moment makes Thomas the first person to realize the depth of Christ's divinity. Until then, the disciples were simply astounded that Christ had risen again. Thomas's response was the first realization of Christ's return to be recorded.

After Jesus appeared to the disciples and showed Thomas His hands and feet, He also appeared to the other disciples, including Thomas, by the Sea of Galilee (John 21). Thomas was also present at the gathering of the disciples in Acts 1, and in Acts 1:21–26 when he and the other disciples chose Matthias as Judas Iscariot's replacement.

After this, Thomas simply vanishes from the Bible. There are no other mentions of Thomas in the New Testament, so we must rely on Christian tradition and other apocryphal texts to fill in the blanks. We find that he extended his ministry into India where he is recognized as the founder of the Syrian Balabar Christians or Christians of St. Thomas.[72] He was supposedly martyred in Madras where the San Thomé Cathedral, his burial place, stands.[73]

Thomas is a prime example of imperfect faith. However, what we can learn from Thomas is invaluable. Jesus reminded him gently that He was the only way to eternity. He reassured Thomas that though he couldn't see Him, Christ was always there with him. His gentle reminders, and even reappearing when Thomas doubted him, should give us hope that even when we flounder in our faith, even when we cannot see what God is doing, He is there. And His gentle reminders are always there as well.

REFLECTION QUESTIONS

When in your own life have you doubted God's goodness for you?

Identify a weakness in yourself, and find a scripture verse to help you with that struggle.

Where does God give us bravery in the Bible? How can we draw on that in our moments of doubting and weakness?

Chapter 9

JAMES, SON OF ALPHAEUS

———— ✻ ————

*T*he ninth disciple is perhaps the most mysterious and confusing of the disciples. The Bible has a habit of repeating names but never clarifying who exactly they are. James, son of Alphaeus is no exception. The New Testament only mentions James in the lists of the 12 disciples and always towards the end, indicating he was less critical than the others.[74] Before we delve into who James the son of Alphaeus (or James the Less as we're going to call him) is, let's look at the five important James figures listed in scripture.

The Five James Figures:

1. James, the son of Zebedee—Apostle, brother of John; also called "James the Greater" (already introduced to him).

2. James, the son of Alphaeus, Apostle—Matthew 10:3; Mark 3:18; Luke 6:15; Acts 1:13

3. James, the brother of the Lord—Matthew 10:3; Mark 6:3; Galatians 1:19. Without a doubt, he must be identified with the James mentioned in Galatians 2:2 and 2:9; Acts 12:17, 15:13 and 21:18; and 1 Corinthians 15:7.

4. James, the son of Mary, brother of Joseph (or Joses)—Mark 15:40 (where he is called "the little", not "the less" or "lesser"); Matthew 27:56. Probably the son of Cleophas or Clopas (found in John 19:25) where "Mary the wife of Cleophas" is mentioned. Married women were distinguished by their husband's names.

5. James, the brother of Jude—Jude 1:1. Catholic scholars identify Jude with the "Brother of James" (Luke 6:16; Acts 1:13) because James was better known in the church.

The church recognizes out of all of these five figures, they all equate to two men. The first James listed is one, and the James's listed in points 2-5 are all grouped together as the second James.

There is etymological evidence that Cleophas is related to the name Alphaeus.[75] We find this supported when we look at the Marys who were at the foot of the cross. Mary of Cleophas is named as the mother of James the Less (the disciple we are looking at). But James the Less is called the son of Alphaeus, thus linking the two names Cleophas and Alphaeus.[76]

All the Jameses in the Bible can be confusing. The consensus is that James the Less, the disciple, is the "James" of 2–5 above. He is also the Bishop of Jerusalem, the author of the book of James in the Bible, and the James who is buried in Rome.[77]

This James is the brother of Jesus (technically his cousin through Joseph and Mary), the son of Cleophas (also Alphaeus, who met Christ on his way to Emmaus and was the brother of Joseph, Mary's husband) and Mary of Alphaeus (sister of the Virgin Mary), the brother of Mary Salome, and the brother of Jude the Apostle called Jude the Less or the Little. This James is also mentioned as "James the Just".[78]

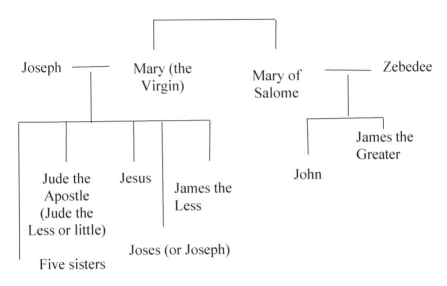

James the Greater is the first James from the list above. The term "Greater" is meant as a means of separating him from James the Less (we find this in Mark 15:40). James the Greater is the James that is most commonly named with Peter, John, and Jesus. If you follow the family tree above, we can see that James the Less and the James's from 2–5 above would be the son of Mary (the Virgin) and Joseph, meaning he is the bother of Jesus.

Let's take a quick side note here and look at the Marys. Biblical scholar and Professor of Ancient Judaism and Early Christianity James Tabor has an interesting theory about the multiple Marys in the Bible. He deduces that "Mary the mother of James and Joses" is the Virgin Mary.[79] This theory means that Mary the mother of Jesus would have had to have married a man named Clopas after her marriage to Joseph. Tabor proposes that a brother of Joseph's would have had to have married his widow in a Levirate marriage.[80]

However, we know for a fact that the Mary of Clopas is *not* the Virgin Mary. The disciple John tells us this in John 19:25: "Standing near the cross was Jesus's mother, and His mother's sister, Mary (the wife of Clopas), and Mary Magdalene." Mary of Clopas could not also be the Virgin Mary in this instance.

If all of these references are to the same person, that would mean that James, the son of Alphaeus, would be the author of the book of James and one of the three men Paul called "pillars" of the church. Some theologians have also argued that James, son of Alphaeus, could be the apostle Matthew's brother.[81] However, we can easily argue against this because the brothers are grouped when they are all listed: James and John, sons of Zebedee, and Simon and Andrew. Matthew is listed first, and when James is listed, he is listed as "James, son of Alphaeus." Matthew is not listed as the son of Alphaeus. The listing of the brothers reflects the belief that these two men were, in fact, not brothers.[82]

At the Crucifixion, all four gospels refer to one of the women present as "the mother of James." Mark 15:40 clarifies that this James is "James the less," leading scholars to believe that it is James, son of Alphaeus, whose mother is being mentioned.[83]

Many modern scholars aren't sure who James the son of Alphaeus, James the Less, or James the brother of Jesus are. Ultimately, there is no true consensus. However, we know that James, son of Alphaeus, and James, son of Zebedee, are *not* the same person.[84]

To clear up some name confusion, let's reflect on the fact that many times in the Bible, people were mentioned by multiple names; Levi is also called Matthew, but they are the same person. Theoretically, James the son of Alphaeus, James the Less, and James the brother of Jesus could all be different people or they could be the same person.

The New Testament lists all twelve disciples in Matthew 10:2–4, Mark 3:14–19, Luke 6:13–16, and Acts 1:13–16. While some of the names are slightly different and the order gets changed, James, son of Alphaeus, is mentioned in these three gospels. He's never mentioned in the Gospel of John, but John never actually lists all twelve disciples. The repeated mention of James means that James spent three years in close union with Jesus, living with Him, witnessing His miracles, and hearing His teachings. He was also privy to multiple demonstrations of Jesus's divinity.

Even though Acts never lists James, he is one of the most influential leaders in the early church.[85] James didn't receive fame or glory while working for Christ. His obscurity in the Bible points not to his identity but his purpose as a disciple. Psalm 115:1 puts it gently. "Not to us, O Lord, not to us, but to your name be the glory…"

James the Less, also called the Lesser, the Younger, the Little, and the Minor is mentioned four times in the Gospels, always following his mother, Mary, who is referred to as Mary of Clopas in John 19:25. Mary of Clopas, if speculation is correct, is the same woman who was at the cross when Jesus was crucified. James the Less is only used once in Mark 15:40, but early Christians used the term to describe the James they were referring to. It's slightly ambiguous, but it's easy to see it was not intended for James the son of Zebedee, one of the most prominent and significant disciples. The connection between James the Less and James the son of Alphaeus is obscure and unknown. However, if we can identify James the son of Alphaeus as James the brother of Jesus, we learn more about his role in the early church.

There's a direct link between James the Less and James the brother of Jesus that would lead us to believe they are the same. Jesus had brothers named James and Joseph, who are mentioned in Mark 6:3 and Matthew 13:55, and James the Less had a brother named Joseph (Mark 15:40). James the brother of Jesus was also known as James the Just, the leader of the church in Jerusalem and the author of the book of James.[86] Paul mentions him in his letter to the Galatians 1:19

> "I saw none of the other apostles—only James, the
> Lord's brother." (Galatians 1:19)

Some theologians argue that because he was listed here in Paul's letter in association with the disciples, James the brother of Jesus and James son of Alphaeus are the same.[87] James the son of Zebedee would not have been described as Jesus's brother, as he would have already been martyred by this time. In Galatians 2 and Acts, Paul describes how James presided over a council to determine whether Gentile believers were following the law of Moses.

> "James, Cephas, and John, these esteemed pillars,
> gave me and Barnabas the right hand of fellowship

when they recognized the grace given to me. They agreed that we should go to the Gentiles, and they to be circumcised." (Galatians 2:9)

Here Paul doesn't refer to James as the brother of Jesus again. This could mean that the James discussed herein is so well known that people would know who Paul is talking about. The early church connects James the brother of Jesus to James the leader of the early church. Whether that is true or not, there is no solid evidence that *this* James is also James the son of Alphaeus, unless James the son of Alphaeus is also James the Less.

If James the son of Alphaeus is also James the Less, we'd have to piece together how the son of Alphaeus and Mary is the brother of Jesus, who was the son of Mary and Joseph through God. Joseph and Mary had four other sons: Joseph, James, Jude, and Simon.[88] They are mentioned in Matthew 12:46 and 13:55, Mark 6:3, John 2:12 and 7:3, 5, and 10, Acts 1:14, 1 Corinthians 9:5, and Galatians 1:19.

Some scholars stress that in the New Testament, there is a distinction between the twelve apostles and the brothers of Christ (Mark 6:3 and Matthew 13:55).[89] James the brother of Christ is mentioned in Galatians 1:19 and is also referred to as James of Jerusalem. We find this in Acts 12:17, 15:13, and 12:18, Galatians

2:9 and 12, and 1 Corinthians 15:7. In 1 Corinthians, we can see the distinction between the twelve and Jesus's brothers.[90]

✳

The Mary described as James's mother in Mark 15:40 and 16:1, Matthew 27:56, and Luke 24:10 is believed to be the Mary of Clopas described in John 19:25. All of these passages list women who were at the foot of the cross when Jesus died. The Gospels all describe this specific Mary as the mother of James; Matthew and Mark also refer to her as the mother of Joseph. The Gospel of John calls her Mary of Clopas and describes her as the sister of Mary, the mother of Jesus (John 19:25).[91] This however is contradictory because what we've learned thus far is that Mary of Clopas was married to Zebedee, and was the half-sister of Mary, meaning that Mary the Virgin could not have been the same woman as Mary of Clopas.

However, it isn't clear if Mary is married to Clopas or is the daughter of Clopas.[92] Scholars originally assumed that Alphaeus was married to Mary, the daughter of Clopas, but other scholars believe that Alphaeus and Clopas are the same people.[93] No matter how you look at Mary, evidence still points to the possibility that James the Less, James the son of Alphaeus, and James the brother of Jesus could all be the same person. Unfortunately, the Bible never explicitly tells us what is true. If James the Just is the same person as James the son of Alphaeus, we are left with multiple people named James listed in the Bible. It's a confusing tangle of identities.

All of the disciples, following the Resurrection, became missionaries somewhere.[94] Where James the son of Alphaeus went is a little fuzzy. The most common notion of how he died was that he was thrown from a pinnacle of the Temple and was beaten and stoned to death, all while praying for his attackers.[95]

Exactly who James the son of Alphaeus remained unclear and very little is known about him. Even so, we can agree on one thing: he was one of the twelve disciples, and being called into ministry personally by Christ is no small feat. Like Peter said in Luke 18:28, "We have left all we had to follow you." His sacrifice to follow Christ does not go unnoticed. Whether he was Jesus's brother or not, Jesus called him into ministry and he followed.

James, though rarely mentioned in the Bible, was still known by the Lord, just as you are known. Our Father has identified us, written us on the palms of His hands, and drawn us to Him. God does not overlook anyone. Jesus didn't overlook James, so have no fear. He will not overlook you.

REFLECTION QUESTIONS

Who was James? We went over a lot in that chapter about who he might or might not be. Who do you think he was? And how does this give you perspective on who you might be?

Do you believe that every person in the Bible plays a significant role in the coming of the kingdom? How do you see yourself fitting into that role?

Where have you been challenged in life? What are some of the struggles you've had to overcome?

Chapter 10

SIMON THE CANAANEAN, CALLED THE ZEALOT

We know very little about the tenth disciple named Simon. He is called Simon the Zealot in the Gospel of Luke and Acts. It is uncertain if he was part of a group called the Zealots, a Jewish nationalistic party, or if the name is an attempt to distinguish him from the disciple Simon Peter.[96]

Some scholars believe Simon was part of the Zealot group, a tax-hating, Roman-hating group. It is believed that Jesus would have chosen Simon to be one of the twelve to counterbalance Matthew, a former tax collector and employee of the Roman Empire.[97] If this is true, it reinforces our preconceived notion that Christ's kingdom is for everyone in all walks of life.[98]

The Zealots usually agreed with the Pharisees, and Jesus

frequently clashed with the Pharisees over their interpretations of the law. We have to wonder what Simon the Zealot thought of that if he was indeed part of the group. The Zealots had a long history in Israel, formed by men who were passionate about obeying the Torah. As people infringed upon their ways, the Zealots sometimes turned to violence.[99] The Zealots included men called Sicarii, or dagger-men, trained assassins who tried to throw off Roman rule.[100] They wandered through large crowds at festivals and other events and used a short curved knife called a Sicarii to kill Romans.[101] The result was the terror that disrupted the Roman government. Whether Simon was actually a part of that group or not, we do not know for sure.

*

In Luke 22:38, the disciples tell Jesus, "See, Lord, here are two swords." Following that, Jesus is arrested in the Garden of Gethsemane. As the story goes on, Peter withdraws his sword and cuts off the ear of the high priest's servant. It wouldn't be too far of a stretch to imagine the second sword belonging to Simon the Zealot. However, he kept it hidden from view as it is never actually mentioned.

The only other references to Simon are in Matthew 10:4, Mark 3:18, Luke 6:15, and Acts 1:13. He was present with the other disciples in the upper room when Jesus appeared after his Ascension. How neat is it that even though it was barely mentioned in the Bible, he was present when the Lord came back? What a gift it was for him to witness Christ's appearance! Though he wasn't mentioned as much as the other disciples, he was never forgotten.

What little we know about Simon the Zealot does not matter when we look at all twelve disciples as a whole. Jesus chose the disciples for particular reasons, and Jesus saw something in Simon the Zealot. He saw an intensity in him that He knew would be used for His purpose in spreading the Gospel. Jesus's kingdom wasn't about politics but salvation. Jesus purposefully picked people who had been fixed on things of the world so he could change their lives and change their outlooks. Jesus came not just to be in the world but also to change the world.

REFLECTION QUESTIONS

Before reading this book, who did you think God was? Has this book shown you a different perspective on His heart?

Do you think everyone deserves to get to Heaven, even the tax collectors or tax haters?

Why do you think Christ chose Simon as one of the twelve if he and Matthew would have conflicted with each other? Is there anyone in the church who conflicts with you?

Can Christians see two sides of the same story? How does that co-exist in the church today?

Chapter 11

JUDE THE SON OF JAMES, ALSO KNOWN AS THADDAEUS

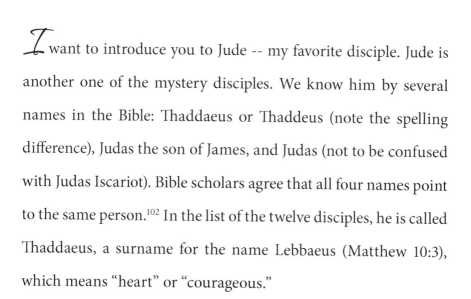

$\mathcal{I}$ want to introduce you to Jude -- my favorite disciple. Jude is another one of the mystery disciples. We know him by several names in the Bible: Thaddaeus or Thaddeus (note the spelling difference), Judas the son of James, and Judas (not to be confused with Judas Iscariot). Bible scholars agree that all four names point to the same person.[102] In the list of the twelve disciples, he is called Thaddaeus, a surname for the name Lebbaeus (Matthew 10:3), which means "heart" or "courageous."

He appears in Matthew 10:3, Mark 3:18, Luke 6:16, John 14:22, and Acts 1:13, and he is possibly the author of the book of Jude.

We know little about his life other than he was probably born and raised in the same area of Galilee as Jesus and the other disciples.

His father was also named Alphaeus, and some scholars believe his brother was James the Less, who we've already looked at in Chapter 9.[103] In Luke, the literal translation of his name Jude means "Jude of James." Originally it was thought that the preposition "of" meant "son of"; however, scholars now believe it means "brother of."[104] Thus, Jude would be the brother of James. If we think Jude the apostle is the same Jude who wrote the book of Jude, we can reason that the James described in Jude 1 refers to James the Just. And because James the Just was Jesus's brother, we can surmise that Jude is a brother to Jesus. It's a stretch, but Matthew 13:55 tells us that Jesus had a brother named Jude, so some biblical scholars use this to connect the three men.

Some scholars believe Jude was born into a Jewish family in Paneas.[105] Others believe his mother was a cousin of Mary, the mother of Jesus, making him a blood relative of Christ even if he was not Christ's brother.[106] We also know that, like the other disciples, he preached following the death of Jesus until his death.[107] Scholars say he preached in Judea, Samaria, Idumaea, Syria, Mesopotamia, and Libya, perhaps alongside Simon the Zealot.

To flesh out some personality and character traits of Jude, we see his skepticism in John 7:5. We read that he doubted Jesus's divinity the first time he learned of it. Remind you of someone else? Doubting Thomas perhaps? Or more like ourselves?

In John 14:22, we see an interaction between Jesus and Jude (Thaddaeus) that reveals a great deal of his character to us. Jude asks Jesus, "Lord, why are you going to reveal yourself only to us and not to the world at large?" (NLT). This is one of the most beautiful pieces of scripture I've read. Why? Because it reveals so much about Jude's character to us! Jude's heart is so big. He has a deep intimate relationship with Christ. He was comfortable enough with Him to ask Him questions in the middle of His teachings. It also shows us Jude was a compassionate person and wanted the whole world to learn of Christ, not just the disciples. The best thing about Jude's character is that he doesn't want to hold Jesus just to himself. He doesn't want anyone to miss out on the riches that Jesus offers.

Like the other disciples, the end of his life is not recorded in the Bible. Christian scholars say that Jude founded a church at Edessa and was crucified, clubbed, or beheaded there as a martyr. Though we find little of his life written in the Bible, Jude shows us a deep passion for his Lord. He lived with Him, worked alongside Him, and preached the Gospel. Jude gave us an idea of what dedication and perseverance look like. He continued Jesus's ministry long after Christ was gone.

REFLECTION QUESTIONS

Have you ever doubted the first time God was good to you? Do you still doubt His goodness?

Jude has compassion for people and for sharing the word. Where do your feelings lie in sharing the Gospel?

Chapter 12
JUDAS ISCARIOT, THE TRAITOR

———— ✳ ————

$\mathcal{W}$e conclude our study of the twelve disciples with perhaps the most well-known disciple, second only to Peter: Judas Iscariot, the traitor. There are eight Judases described in the Bible but only one of them is the one we're looking at here.

1. Judas Iscariot, the betrayer of Jesus and one of the apostles (Matthew 10:4)

2. Judas the son of James, also one of the twelve apostles (Luke 6:16)

3. Judas the brother of Jesus (Matthew 13:55)

4. Judas, Paul's host in Damascus (Acts 9:11)

5. Judas, called Barsabbas, companion of Paul and the leading Christian leader in Jerusalem (Acts 15:22)

6. Judas, a revolutionary leader (Acts 5:27)

7. Judah, an unknown person in the genealogy of Jesus (Luke 3:30)

8. And Judah, son of Jacob in Jesus's genealogy and ancestor of an Israelite tribe (Matthew 1:2, Revelation 7:5)[108]

Judas is sometimes referred to as Judas, son of Simon (John 6:71, 13:2, and 13:26), but is most commonly known as Judas Iscariot (Matthew 10:4; Mark 3:19; Luke 6:16). The name Iscariot has several different definitions, and if you're anything like me, you grew up believing it meant traitor. However, Joshua 15:25 tells us it most likely means "man of Kerioth," after a town inhabited by the tribe of Judah.[109] The best estimation today would be to equate Kerioth with Kerioth-Hezron (Joshua 15:25), which is fifteen miles south of Hebron. Judas was the only apostle from Judea; the rest were from Galilee.[110]

Judas doesn't seem to have been called by Jesus into ministry like Philip, Nathanael, or Peter, but Judas is listed as one of the twelve from the very beginning (Mark 3:19). He also isn't mentioned as often as some of the other disciples, but in John 12:6 and John 13:29, we find out he was the disciples' treasurer.[111] This position in turn enabled Judas to use his position for personal gain. He was not an honest man when Jesus found him. John 12:6 tells us that "he was a thief; as keeper of the money bag, he used to help himself." He was, in many ways, a politician. If that made you wrinkle your nose, I feel you. I did the same. He had power by being a follower of Christ, and it allowed him liberties that he took advantage of. We witness this greed in John 12. Here Judas protests Jesus's actions at a famous dinner. This is the dinner where Jesus's friend Mary, sister to Lazurus and Martha, takes her perfume and pours it on Jesus's feet in the act of worship.

Let's look at the history of this event a little more in-depth. The honorific process of washing Jesus's feet with perfume is also recorded in all four gospels. The accounts in Matthew 26, Mark 14, and John 12 all locate the event in Bethany, a city in the south. In the Gospel of Luke, the dinner is held in the north and features an unknown sinful woman. We know this because Luke 7 indicates Jesus was ministering in the northern areas of Nain and Capernaum.

Regarding Judas, we need to remember the period when this was taking place. During this time, perfume was a costly item. Perfumes were made out of natural oils, and the oil used often increased a perfume's rarity. Perfumes during this time were used for religious purposes, such as rituals or burials, for medicinal purposes, or for cosmetic purposes.

Knowing this, what Judas does suddenly should make sense. His actions and words about the perfume in John 12 show us a glimpse of the greed we most often associate with him. He protests to Christ, asking why the money used to buy the perfume wasn't going to the poor instead of being wasted (John 12:5). Though his intentions here seem sincere and could be seen as such if asked by a different disciple, John 12:6 tells us that Judas intended to skim the money from the money bag for himself as he did not care for the poor and was a thief. Rather than expose Judas, Jesus uses the moment to tell his disciples of his impending death.

> "You will always have the poor among you, but you
> will not always have me." (John 12:7–8)

The pouring of perfume is the tipping point for Judas. Immediately following this scene, Matthew and Mark describe Judas making his deal with the Pharisees (Matthew 26:14–16; Mark 14:10–21). This scene is not defined in the other two gospels but is still there. In the Gospel of John, we see Judas sitting at the table next to Christ in 13:26–28. Jesus dips bread into his cup and hands it to Judas, telling him, "what you are about to do, do quickly."[112] Jesus knew what Judas was doing. Yet Judas still chose to follow through with it. Imagine the greed and lowliness Judas must have felt to keep through with what he was going to do.

He leaves the meal immediately, and we follow Judas to the Garden of Gethsemane. Matthew 26:48 describes the scene where Judas kisses Christ on the cheek, marking him as the Messiah so the guards can arrest him.

Picture the moment Judas realized what he'd done. The guards seize Jesus and his friend is suddenly taken away. In Matthew 27, we see Judas's remorse and decline. We tangibly feel his grief as he realizes what he has done. He is bitter, broken and sad. In Matthew 27:3, we see Judas take the silver back to the chief priests and elders and attempt to return it. He was at fault for the death of an innocent man. Jesus had chosen him to be one of His closest friends, yet Judas betrayed Him to a gruesome death. When he cannot return the silver to the Pharisees, they laugh at him. They laugh at his sorrow and the admittance of his sin. Only Jesus did not condemn him. Even when He knew what Judas was going to do. There is no satisfaction in anything this world can offer us, and Judas suddenly realizes that.

Realizing his mistake, Judas throws the silver at their feet, rushes away, and hangs himself.

Judas' Timeline of Betrayal

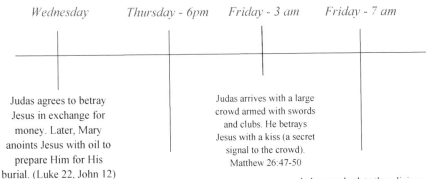

| *Wednesday* | *Thursday - 6pm* | *Friday - 3 am* | *Friday - 7 am* |

Judas agrees to betray Jesus in exchange for money. Later, Mary anoints Jesus with oil to prepare Him for His burial. (Luke 22, John 12)

Judas arrives with a large crowd armed with swords and clubs. He betrays Jesus with a kiss (a secret signal to the crowd). Matthew 26:47-50

During Passover, Jesus humbly washes the disciples' feet. He then states, " ... one of you will betray Me," speaking of Judas. John 13

Judas goes back to the religious leaders because he realized his mistake. , "I have sinned and betrayed innocent blood." He throws the money, runs away and hangs himself. Matthew 27

Though Judas's life was tragic, and potentially the most heart-wrenching of all the disciples, God can still be seen and exemplified through him. Judas made the greatest mistake. But his sorrow does not outweigh God's love for us.

We already know about the prediction of Jesus's death and Judas's betrayal in Zechariah 11:12–14, Psalm 41:9, and John 13:18. We are given the story of a man who betrayed Jesus but was still deeply loved by him. Jesus knew from the very beginning that Judas was going to betray Him, yet He still opened His arms, invited Judas in, and asked him to follow Him. Just like Jesus is waiting to take us into his arms. No matter our mistakes, no matter our faults. Jesus is waiting on us!

Our Father takes everything that was meant for evil and turns it for good. The death of Christ was meant to silence the church, but instead, it fulfilled the plan that God had laid out long before man could interfere. God's purpose far outweighs the world's plans.

REFLECTION QUESTIONS

Judas is possibly the most famous disciple in the Bible. Have you ever had a Judas Iscariot moment, a moment when you traded Christ for something better?

Have you ever done something in your life you instantly regretted? How did you fix it?

Jesus knew Judas was going to betray Him from the beginning. Yet He still extended his arms and His love for Judas. Have you seen someone act like Jesus in this situation? Or have you seen someone be Judas, welcomed even though he or she continued to cause pain? How can you pray for that person?

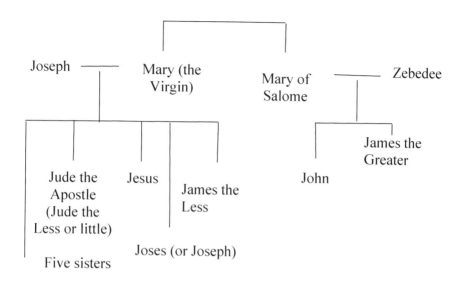

Judas' Timeline of Betrayal

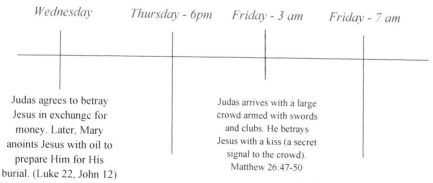

Wednesday   *Thursday - 6pm*   *Friday - 3 am*   *Friday - 7 am*

Judas agrees to betray Jesus in exchange for money. Later, Mary anoints Jesus with oil to prepare Him for His burial. (Luke 22, John 12)

Judas arrives with a large crowd armed with swords and clubs. He betrays Jesus with a kiss (a secret signal to the crowd). Matthew 26:47-50

During Passover, Jesus humbly washes the disciples' feet. He then states, " ... one of you will betray Me," speaking of Judas. John 13

Judas goes back to the religious leaders because he realized his mistake. , "I have sinned and betrayed innocent blood." He throws the money, runs away and hangs himself. Matthew 27

Follow-up

The lives and stories of the 12 Disciples paint a picture of Jesus's character. In different ways, we each walk our own path to salvation. The end goal is ultimately the same, but the way we get there is not. Jesus recognized this when He chose the men He did to follow Him. Bearing our cross is not easy. But for Jesus it is the only worth while thing this world brings us.

My hope for you is that some aspect of this book spoke to your heart and encouraged you. May you find endurance within these pages to keep seeking the ultimate treasure, like Matthew 6:19-21 (CSB) tells us. "Don't store up for yourselves treasures on earth, where moth and rust destory and where thieves break in and steal. But store up for yourselves treasures in heaven, where neither moth nor rust destroys, and where thieves don't break in and steal. For where your treasure is, there your heart will be also."

As Christians, our yokes are light, and our burdens easy. As long as we walk in the way of Christ. May you do that always.

Acknowledgements

Thank you to all the friends and family whose efforts, love and support encouraged me to write this book. I wouldn't have done it without you. There is a list of people this book wouldn't have happened if it wasn't for.

Specifically, thank you to L. Swigart for writing on one of my poems in seventh grade that I could be a writer. Here I am. To A. Schneider who told me in tenth grade that I could teach others what I know. I can, and it's because of you. Thank you to my college professor who told me I couldn't write -- you motivated me to prove you wrong.

Thank you to the people that read and reread this book, helping me make it the best book that it could be. I couldn't have done it without you.

Thank you to my sisters for always keeping me in endless supply of notebooks to keep filling with never finished stories. Cheers to you, because I finally finished one. My dearest brother -- our golf cart rides were made of dreams and this was one of them. To my parents, my greatest accomplishment was being your daughter. And to my husband, thank you for supporting all of my many dreams. Your love for me and Jesus kept seeing me through. Thank you.

Notes

1. Daniel William O'Connor, "Saint Peter the Apostle," in *Encyclopædia Britannica*, updated February 19, 2020, https://www.britannica.com/biography/Saint-Peter-the-Apostle.
2. O'Connor, "Saint Peter the Apostle."
3. Jerome Murphy-O'Connor, "Peter's House," Bible Odyssey, updated March 12, 2019, https://www.bibleodyssey.org/en/places/related-articles/peters-house.
4. O'Connor, "Saint Peter the Apostle."
5. Jeffrey Hays, "St. Peter: His Life, Leadership, Death and Relationship with Jesus," Facts and Details, updated September 2018, http://factsanddetails.com/world/cat55/ sub391/entry-5759.html.
6. O'Connor, "Saint Peter the Apostle."
7. Allacin Morimizu, "Allacin's Free Illustrated Summaries of Christian Classics: Illustrated Summary of Twelve Ordinary Men (the Apostles) by John MacArthur," Allacin's Free Illustrated Summaries of Christian Classics, updated April 24, 2018, https://allacin.blogspot.com/2018/04/illustrated-summary-of-twelve-ordinary.html.
8. Murphy-O'Connor, "Peter's House."
9. O'Connor, "Saint Peter the Apostle."
10. Daniel William O'Connor, "Saint Peter the Apostle," in *Encyclopædia Britannica*, updated February 19, 2020, https://www.britannica.com/biography/Saint-Peter-the-Apostle.
11. Ibid
12. Knox Church (EPC). 2022. Andrew: Apostle and Evangelist. [online] Available at: https://knoxepc.wordpress.com/2020/08/26/andrew-apostle-and-evangelist/ Accessed 25 August 2022.
13. Christopher Muscato, "Andrew the Apostle: Biography, Facts & Death—Video & Lesson Transcript," Study, updated November 2, 2020, https://study.com/academy/lesson/andrew-the-apostle-biography-facts-death.html.

14. Ryan Nelson, "Who Was Andrew the Apostle? The Beginner's Guide," Overview Bible, June 17, 2019, https://overviewbible.com/andrew-the-apostle/.

15. Ibid

16. Jack Wellman, "The Apostle Andrew Biography, Life and Death," What Christians Want to Know, https://www.whatchristianswanttoknow.com/the-apostle-andrew-biography-life-and-death/.

17. Ibid

18. Ibid

19. Michael T.R.B. Turnbull, "Saint Andrew," BBC, updated July 31, 2009, https://www.bbc.co.uk/religion/religions/christianity/saints/andrew.shtml#:~:text=Andrew.

20. Ibid

21. Jack Wellman, "The Apostle Andrew Biography, Life and Death," What Christians Want to Know, https://www.whatchristianswanttoknow.com/the-apostle-andrew-biography-life-and-death/.

22. Christopher Muscato, "Andrew the Apostle: Biography, Facts & Death—Video & Lesson Transcript," Study, updated November 2, 2020, https://study.com/academy/lesson/andrew-the-apostle-biography-facts-death.html.

23. Ryan Nelson, "Who Was Andrew the Apostle? The Beginner's Guide," Overview Bible, June 17, 2019, https://overviewbible.com/andrew-the-apostle/.

24. Ibid

25. Ibid

26. Ibid

27. Michael T.R.B. Turnbull, "Saint Andrew," BBC, updated July 31, 2009, https://www.bbc.co.uk/religion/religions/christianity/saints/andrew.shtml#:~:text=Andrew.

28. Ibid

29. Ibid

30. Ibid

31. Jack Zavada, "Meet The Apostle James: First Apostle to Die for Jesus," Learn Religions, updated December 7, 2020, https://www.learnreligions.com/profile-of-apostle-james-701062.

32. Editors of Encyclopædia Britannica, "Saint James," in Encyclopædia Britannica, updated January 8, 2021, https://www.britannica.com/biography/Saint-James-son-of-Zebedee.

33. Maria Nerushenko, "Get to Know the 12 Disciples of Jesus Christ: Apostle #3, James the Elder," The Talkative Man, updated March 2, 2017, https://www.talkativeman.com/ apostle-james-the-elder/.

34. Hays, Jeffrey. "Apostles after the Death of Jesus." Facts and Details. Accessed August 24, 2022.

35. The Catholic Periodical and Literature Index. 1999. https://overviewbible.com/saint-james/

36. Ibid

37. Henry Chadwick, "Saint John the Apostle," in *Encyclopædia Britannica*, updated January 8, 2021, https://www.britannica.com/biography/Saint-John-the-Apostle.

38. Ibid

39. Ibid

40. "1539. 'The Disciple Whom Jesus Loved.' | Answers in Genesis." n.d. Accessed August 24, 2022. https://answersingenesis.org/education/spurgeon-sermons/1539-the-disciple-whom-jesus-loved/.https://answersingenesis.org/education/spurgeon-sermons/1539-the-disciple-whom-jesus-loved/

41. "Why Did the Apostle John Refer to Himself As, "the Disciple Whom .." n.d. Accessed August 24, 2022. https://stjohnoneone.com/2013/04/02/why-did-the-apostle-john-refer-to-himself-as-the-disciple-whom-jesus-loved/.

42. Marion Santiago, "Saint James: His Biography According to the Bible," Santiago in Love, July 2, 2020, http://santiagoinlove.com/en/st-james-biography-bible/.

43. Zavada, "Meet The Apostle James."

44. Henry Chadwick, "Saint John the Apostle," in *Encyclopædia Britannica*, updated January 8, 2021, https://www.britannica.com/biography/Saint-John-the-Apostle.

45. "How Did Apostle John Die?" n.d. Accessed August 28, 2022. https://www.biblestudy.org/question/how-did-apostle-john-die.html.

46. Chadwick, "Saint John the Apostle."

47. Harold W. Attridge, "The Apostle John," Bible Odyssey, December 9, 2021, https://www.bibleodyssey.org/en/people/main-articles/apostle-john.

48.

49. Ibid

50. Attridge, "The Apostle John."

51. Jack Zavada, "Philip the Apostle–Follower of Jesus Christ," Learn Religions, updated June 10, 2018, https://www.learnreligions.com/philip-the-apostle-follower-of-jesus-701070.

52. Ibid

53. "Not Counting Women and Children - Reformed Journal." n.d. Accessed August 24, 2022. https://reformedjournal.com/not-counting-women-children/.

54. Zavada, "Philip the Apostle."

55. Ibid

56. The Catholic Periodical and Literature Index. 1999. https://www.stiltonchurches.com/about1-coez

57. Bruce Alderman, "What Is the Significance of Jesus Seeing Nathanael under the Fig Tree?", Christianity Stack Exchange, accessed October 30, 2021, https://christianity.stackexchange.com/questions/1656/what-is-the-significance-of-jesus-seeing-nathanael-under-the-fig-tree.

58. "Saint Bartholomew - New World Encyclopedia." n.d. Accessed August 25, 2022. https://www.newworldencyclopedia.org/entry/Saint_Bartholomew.

59. "Bartholomew the Apostle," People Pill, accessed October 30, 2021, https://peoplepill.com/people/bartholomew-the-apostle/.

60. "Bartholomew the Apostle."

61. Ibid

62. Biography.com editors, "Saint Bartholomew," Biography, updated April 8, 2021, https://www.biography.com/religious-figure/saint-bartholomew.

63. "Gospel of Matthew: Themes and Emphases." n.d. Accessed August 25, 2022. https://catholic-resources.org/Bible/Matthew-LiteraryFeatures.htm.

64. "'Monetary System, Taxation, and Publicans in the Time of Christ' by .." n.d. Accessed August 25, 2022. https://egrove.olemiss.edu/aah_journal/vol13/iss2/11/.

65. Jack Zavada, "Meet Matthew the Apostle, Ex-Tax Collector," Learn Religions, updated August 14, 2020, https://www.learnreligions.com/matthew-tax-collector-and-apostle-701067.

66. Ibid

67. Ibid

68. "Saint Matthew | History, Facts, Feast Day, & Death | Britannica." n.d. Accessed August 25, 2022. https://www.britannica.com/biography/Saint-Matthew.

69. "How Did the Apostles Die? What We Actually Know - OverviewBible." n.d. Accessed August 25, 2022. https://overviewbible.com/how-did-the-apostles-die/.

70. Jack Zavada, "Meet Matthew the Apostle, Ex-Tax Collector," Learn Religions, updated August 14, 2020, https://www.learnreligions.com/matthew-tax-collector-and-apostle-701067.

71. Jack Zavada, "Meet Matthew the Apostle, Ex-Tax Collector," Learn Religions, updated August 14, 2020, https://www.learnreligions.com/matthew-tax-collector-and-apostle-701067.

72. Editors of *Encyclopædia Britannica*, "St. Thomas," in *Encyclopædia Britannica,* updated January 1, 2021, https://www.britannica.com/biography/Saint-Thomas.
73. Ibid
74. Ibid
75. Father Ryan Erlenbush, "Keeping Them Straight: James the Greater and James the Less"
76. Ibid
77. Ibid
78. Admin, "Did Mary Have Any Children Other than Jesus? If So, How Can She Be the Eternal Virgin?", Bible.org, accessed October 30, 2021, https://bible.org/question/did-mary-have-any-children-other-jesus-if-so-how-can-she-be-eternal-virgin.
79. Father Ryan Erlenbush, "Keeping Them Straight: James the Greater and James the Less", The New Theological Movement, updated July 25, 2011. http://newtheologicalmovement.blogspot.com/2011/07/keeping-them-straight-james-greater-and.html
80. Ryan Nelson, "Who Was James Son of Alphaeus? The Beginner's Guide," Overview Bible, September 12, 2019, https://overviewbible.com/james-son-of-alphaeus/
81. Ryan Nelson, "Who Was James Son of Alphaeus? The Beginner's Guide," Overview Bible, September 12, 2019, https://overviewbible.com/james-son-of-alphaeus/.
82. "James (Son of Alphaeus), St.", Encyclopedia, accessed October 30, 2021, https://www.encyclopedia.com/religion/encyclopedias-almanacs-transcripts-and-maps/james-son-alphaeus-st
83. Ibid
84. Ryan Nelson, "Who Was James Son of Alphaeus? The Beginner's Guide," Overview Bible, September 12, 2019, https://overviewbible.com/james-son-of-alphaeus/.
85. "James the Less: The Obscure Apostle of Christ." n.d. Accessed August 25, 2022. https://www.learnreligions.com/james-the-less-obscure-apostle-701076.
86. Ryan Nelson, "Who Was James Son of Alphaeus? The Beginner's Guide," Overview Bible, September 12, 2019, https://overviewbible.com/james-son-of-alphaeus/.
87. Ibid
88. "Bible Lesson Online Research Tools." n.d. Accessed August 25, 2022. http://www.bibletexts.com/glossary/.

89. Father Ryan Erlenbush, "Keeping Them Straight: James the Greater and James the Less"

90. Editors of *Encyclopædia Britannica*, "St. Thomas," in *Encyclopædia Britannica,* updated January 1, 2021, https://www.britannica.com/biography/Saint-Thomas.

91. Ryan Nelson, "Who Was James Son of Alphaeus? The Beginner's Guide," Overview Bible, September 12, 2019, https://overviewbible.com/james-son-of-alphaeus/.

92. "Mary of Cleophas | EWTN." n.d. Accessed August 25, 2022. https://www.ewtn.com/catholicism/library/mary-of-cleophas-1080.

93. "Topical Bible: Alphaeus." n.d. Accessed August 25, 2022. https://biblehub.com/topical/a/alphaeus.htm.

94. "The First Christian Missionaries - World History Encyclopedia." n.d. Accessed August 25, 2022. https://www.worldhistory.org/article/1658/the-first-christian-missionaries/.

95. Ryan Nelson, "Who Was James Son of Alphaeus? The Beginner's Guide," Overview Bible, September 12, 2019, https://overviewbible.com/james-son-of-alphaeus/.

96. "James (Son of Alphaeus), St.", Encyclopedia, accessed October 30, 2021, https://www.encyclopedia.com/religion/encyclopedias-almanacs-transcripts-and-maps/james-son-alphaeus-st

97. Jack Zavada, "Meet Simon the Zealot: A Mystery Apostle." Learn Religions, updated July 17, 2018, https://www.learnreligions.com/simon-the-zealot-mystery-apostle-701071.

98. Ibid

99. Editors of *Encyclopædia Britannica*, "St. Simon the Apostle," in *Encyclopædia Britannica,* updated May 6, 2020, https://www.britannica.com/biography/Saint-Simon-the-Apostle.

100. Jack Zavada, "Meet Simon the Zealot: A Mystery Apostle." Learn Religions, updated July 17, 2018, https://www.learnreligions.com/simon-the-zealot-mystery-apostle-701071.

101. Ibid

102. Editors of *Encyclopædia Britannica*, "St. Simon the Apostle," in *Encyclopædia Britannica,* updated May 6, 2020, https://www.britannica.com/biography/Saint-Simon-the-Apostle.

103. "Thaddaeus (Judas, Son of James) the Apostle." n.d. Accessed August 25, 2022. http://www.aboutbibleprophecy.com/p155.htm.

104. "Who Was Jude the Apostle? The Beginner." n.d. Accessed August 25, 2022. https://overviewbible.com/jude-the-apostle/.

105. "Jude the Apostle - New World Encyclopedia." n.d. Accessed August 25, 2022. https://www.newworldencyclopedia.org/entry/Jude_the_Apostle.

106. Ibid

107. Ibid

108. Ibid

109. George E. Meisinger, "Judas," Bible.org, accessed October 30, 2021, https://bible.org/article/judas.

110. Ibid

111. "Judas Iscariot," Bible Study Tools, accessed October 30, 2021, https://www.biblestudytools.com/dictionary/judas-iscariot/.

112. Meisinger, "Judas."

113. Ibid

Printed in the United States
by Baker & Taylor Publisher Services